OHIO COUNTY
WHEELING,

P9-EMP-054

THE COMPASS

OHIO COUNTY PUBLIC LIBRARY
WHEELING, W. VA. 26003

INVENTIONS THAT CHANGED OUR LIVES

THE COMPASS

By Paula Z. Hogan

Illustrated by David Wool

J
629.045
Hoga
1982

WALKER AND COMPANY New York

SEP 14 1983   250668

Thanks are due to Professor David Woodward, Department of Geography, University of Wisconsin, for checking the text and illustrations of this book.

Library of Congress Cataloging in Publication Data

Hogan, Paula Z.
  The compass.

  Includes index.
  Summary: Traces the history of the compass from its
invention by the ancient Chinese through its use by
early explorers to modern uses and developments.
  1. Compass—History—Juvenile literature. [1. Compass.
2. Voyages and travels] I. Wool, David, ill.
II. Title.
VK577.H58   1982   629.04'5   82-70439
ISBN 0-8027-6452-5   AACR2
ISBN 0-8027-6453-3 (lib. bdg.)

Text Copyright © 1982 by PAULA Z. HOGAN
Illustrations Copyright © 1982 by DAVID WOOL

All rights reserved. No part of this book may be reproduced or transmitted in any form or by any means, electric or mechanical, including photocopying, recording, or by any information storage and retrieval system, without permission in writing from the Publisher.

First published in the United States of America in 1982 by the Walker Publishing Company, Inc.

Published simultaneously in Canada by John Wiley & Sons Canada, Limited, Rexdale, Ontario.

ISBN: 0-8027-6452-5 Trade
      0-8027-6453-3 Reinf.

Library of Congress Catalog Card Number: 82-70439

Printed in the United States of America

Book designed by LENA FONG HOR
10 9 8 7 6 5 4 3 2 1

CONTENTS

1

The Chinese Invention

FOR LONG CENTURIES sailors took bearings from the wind, sun, and stars. But wind could become an enemy. It blew clouds and fog across the sky, hiding the stars. High winds and stormy seas drove ships off course. Rumors told of monsters lurking at the edges of the earth. The real killers were hunger and thirst as ships drifted, lost on the open ocean.

Seamen needed a tool to find their way. It had to work on the darkest of nights and in the worst of storms; in the tropics as well as the frozen Arctic seas. The tool is the *magnetic compass*. With map and compass sailors warned one another of sunken reefs and steady winds. They could pinpoint their own position and choose the safest route to port. The compass is a simple tool that changed the history of the world. Its story begins in ancient China with magicians playing chess.

Two thousand years ago a magician was called to the royal palace. The emperor was bored and demanded amusement. If the magician failed to entertain him, the emperor would cut off his head. The magician's name was Luan Ta. He was a clever man who knew many tricks. But the emperor had seen every trick in Asia. Luan Ta had only one hope, his fighting chess men.

Luan Ta bowed before the emperor and arranged his figures on the board. At once the chess pieces came alive, moving this way and that, crashing into each other! The emperor clapped his hands with delight and Luan Ta lived to be a fat old man.

What does a game like chess have to do with the magnetic compass? Long ago chess was a different game played for a different purpose. Figures stood for the five elements: air, wood, fire, metal, and water. Other pieces stood for the wind, sun, and stars. Tossed on a board like pickup sticks, their positions were supposed to foretell the future.

One chess piece was shaped like a spoon. It stood for the Big Dipper, a constellation of stars. People of the ancient world knew that a line drawn through the last two stars of the Dipper points to the North Star. Chinese magicians made a wonderful discovery. The spoon-shaped piece also pointed north! It didn't matter if it was night or day, on land or sea, in the deepest cave or on the highest mountain—the piece always turned to the north. What did matter was the kind of metal from which the spoon was made.

The last two stars of the Big Dipper point to the North Star.

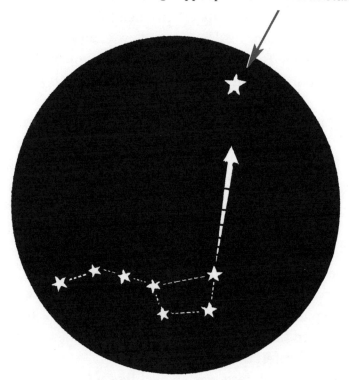

The Chinese called it "tzu shih" or "loving stone." We know it as lodestone, an iron ore found in nature. Lodestone is magnetic. A magnet is any rock or metal that draws bits of iron to its surface. Iron becomes magnetic when it is rubbed against a lodestone.

Experiment

FIND OUT ABOUT MAGNETISM

Use a magnet to pick up a nail, a needle, and a paper clip. You can buy a cheap magnet or you can use the magnetic clips or hooks most kitchens have. Will a magnet pick up a pencil or a plastic toy? Try a toothpick or a pin. Pennies and nickels are not made of iron. What happens when you try to pick up coins with a magnet? Only iron or steel objects will be picked up by a magnet.

The first compass was a lodestone spoon turning on a plate.

Chinese legends tell of palaces defended by lodestone walls. Enemies carrying weapons of iron were stopped at the gates. Sailors warned of lodestone islands that pulled nails from ships' planks, drowning all aboard. Luan Ta, the wise magician, saved his head by using lodestone chess pieces. When he mixed them with iron figures, they drew together.

The Chinese thought that magnets pointed north because they were "afraid" of fire. They linked fire with the south where the climate is hot. Fire melts iron, so magnets spun away from the south.

Today we have other ideas to explain why magnets point north. Every magnet has two *poles*. One is called the north pole and the other is called the south pole.

Lines of force flow from the north pole to the south pole, forming a *magnetic field*.

The earth is a very large magnet. Like all other magnets, it has a north and a south magnetic pole. Lines of force flow from the earth's north magnetic pole to its south magnetic pole. These lines form the earth's magnetic field.

Like poles repel. The north pole of a magnet will push away the north pole of another magnet. Opposite poles attract. The north pole of one magnet will pull toward the south pole of another magnet. So the south pole of a magnet points north because it is attracted to the earth's north magnetic pole.

Opposite poles attract. Like poles repel.

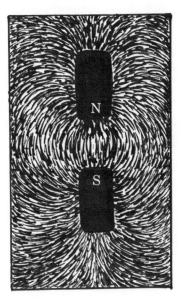 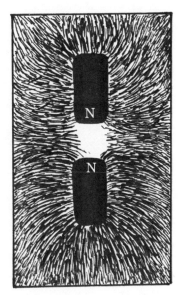

Even a strong magnet cannot point north if it is very heavy or resting on a rough surface. The Chinese invented compasses that solved these problems.

The first compass was a lodestone spoon. It turned on a mirror-smooth board called a heaven plate. The heaven plate rested on a square earth plate. Both plates carried magical markings for the four directions.

Magicians made another compass by sealing lodestone inside a wooden turtle. They forced a needle through the tail end until it struck the lodestone. As the turtle turned on a sharpened bamboo pin, the needle marked north.

The Chinese turtle compass

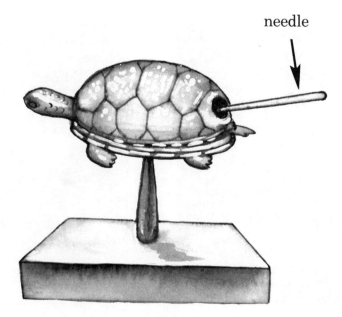

needle

The Chinese invented another simple compass by hanging a magnetic needle from a silk thread. Protected from wind, the needle spun around until it rested in a north-south direction.

Experiment

MAKE A CHINESE HANGING COMPASS

Rub one end of a magnet along a needle. Always rub in the same direction. If you do this 20 to 30 times, the needle will become magnetic. To test its magnetism, see if the needle will pick up a pin.

Tie one end of a *short* thread around the center of your magnetized needle. Tie the other end around a pencil. Place the pencil across the rim of a glass wide enough to let the needle swing freely when you lower it into the glass. When it comes to rest, the needle will point in a north-south direction.

The first liquid compass was a magnetic iron shaving in the shape of a fish. The fish floated in a bowl of water. Compass-makers replaced the fish with a floating needle which showed directions more clearly.

Since iron loses its magnetism, the Chinese experimented with other metals. They heated iron and carbon together to make steel. Steel is stronger than iron and less likely to rust. Compass needles are made from steel because it holds magnetism for a long time.

At last the Chinese had a dependable compass, but they still needed lodestone to magnetize their needles. In A.D. 1000 they discovered a new way to make magnets. The Chinese set glowing steel bars in a north-south direction and cooled them in a vat of water. The steel became magnetic because it was in line with the earth's magnetic field and cooled quickly. Lodestone was unnecessary.

The Chinese made other discoveries such as paper and printing presses which helped scientists record their ideas. Astronomers wrote compass readings on paper and sent printed copies to other scientists. When astronomers shared their ideas, they discovered that compass needles do not point due north. In some places they point a little to the northeast and in other places they point to the northwest. We call this discovery *declination*.

Declination occurs because the earth's magnetic poles are over 1,000 miles from the geographic poles. A compass needle always points to the magnetic North Pole. The difference between the magnetic North Pole

N   S

Chinese floating compass

and the geographic North Pole is called declination.

The Chinese used the compass to plan for the future, build cities, and study the stars. China's sailors seldom used the compass. Their ships stayed close to shore.

The names of early compass-makers are not recorded. Chinese civilization valued the invention, not the inventor. But the genius and skill of these unknown compass-makers changed the course of history.

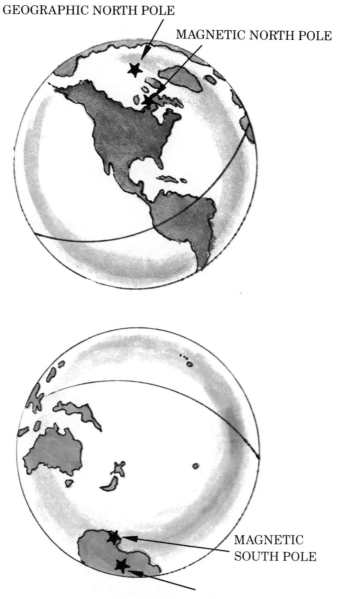

GEOGRAPHIC NORTH POLE

MAGNETIC NORTH POLE

MAGNETIC
SOUTH POLE

GEOGRAPHIC SOUTH POLE

2

The Compass on Ships

FAR TO THE WEST, in Lebanon, the ancient Phoenicians were the greatest nagivators in the world. From the heart of their empire they set up trading posts along the Mediterranean coast. In Spain a 2,000-year-old compass bowl has been found. It is painted with Phoenician letters to mark direction.

Phoenician letters mark directions at the bottom of this 2,000-year-old compass bowl.

N

W   E

S

Experiment

MAKE A PHOENICIAN FLOATING COMPASS

Rub one end of a magnet along a needle. Rub in the same direction toward the point. You should do this about 25 times to make the needle magnetic. Then pass the needle through a cork until it balances when you float it in the water. See which end of the needle points north. Is it the pointed end or the "eye" end? Check it against a store-bought compass.

Then mark the letter "N" on one side of a deep bowl. Write your letter near the rim. Write the letter "S" directly across from the "N." Write the letter "E" on the right side of the bowl, halfway between "N" and "S." Write the letter "W" directly across from "E."

Fill your bowl half full of water. Float the needle and cork in the bowl. Turn the bowl so that the north end of the needle points to the letter "N."

WATCH THE POLES ATTRACT AND REPEL

Magnetize another needle by rubbing with a magnet 25 times towards the point. Now place the pointed end of this needle close to the pointed end of the first one floating in the water. They are like poles and the needle will move away. Now try the "eye" end of the needle by putting it close to the pointed end of the floating needle. Notice how the poles attract each other.

When the Phoenicians were conquered, the Greeks took control of the Mediterranean trade. Greek sailors found their way by the "feel of the wind." A wind from the north felt cold and one from the south felt warm. By day they watched the sun rise in the east and set in the west. At night they steered by the stars. Seamen knew every constellation in the sky. The Big Dipper lies to the north. Navigators kept the Dipper "at their left hand" when they sailed east. As long as the skies were clear, Greek ships crisscrossed the Mediterranean. In fogs they dropped anchor until fair weather returned.

Greek tales never tell of the magnetic compass, but stories of lodestone were known. In one legend a simple shepherd tended his sheep. He leaned on an iron-tipped staff as he hiked up and down the mountainside. One day he rested his staff on a pile of rocks. To his surprise

Greek warship

the shepherd had to pull with both hands to free his staff. The shepherd lived near the city of Magnesia. To this day all rocks that attract iron are named for that city. They are called magnets.

By A.D. 300 Greek and Roman civilization was in

ruins. For the next six hundred years Europe was attacked by wandering tribes. They burned schools, libraries, and books. Europe entered the Dark Ages and learning came to a standstill.

During the Dark Ages southern Europeans seldom sailed far from shore. But the Northmen, or Vikings, roamed far and wide on the open sea. Like the Greeks they were guided by the wind and stars. The flight paths of birds often led them to land. Vikings crossed the North Atlantic, reaching America. Storms, icebergs, and bitter cold did not stand in their way.

Middle Eastern sailors never lost their skill in navigation. Beginning in A.D. 600 the Arabs raised a powerful empire. Their lands stretched across North Africa into southern Spain and France. The Arabs navigated by the stars and marked direction with the magnetic compass.

The tribes of Europe became Christian and settled down around A.D. 1000. Peace gave men time to study and learn. European kings led their soldiers on crusades to the Middle East. Fighting battle after battle with the Arabs, the Christians lost every crusade. But they learned a great deal from their Arab enemies. The Arabs were expert mathematicians and astronomers. They taught the Europeans to build better ships and steer a straighter course. European seamen learned of the magnetic compass. Soon every ship carried one on board.

Alexander Neckham was the first European to write about the compass. In A.D. 1187 he described a floating reed pierced by a magnetic needle. Neckham also wrote about a dry compass needle turning on a pivot. The pivot was usually a nail driven upward through the bottom of a wooden bowl. Neckham explained that sailors only used the compass on cloudy nights. In clear weather they navigated by the wind and stars.

In the 1100s people thought lodestone had magical powers. Some believed it would cure the sick. Onions and garlic were said to demagnetize lodestone. Sailors didn't eat vegetables in case their breath ruined compass needles.

The ship's navigator was known as a *pilot*. He magnetized his compass needle by rubbing it against a lodestone. Sometimes the pilot would amaze young seamen with a show of magic. He would float an unmagnetized needle in a bowl of water. Holding the lodestone close to the rim, he moved it around and around. The needle followed because it was close enough to the lodestone to become magnetic. Suddenly the pilot snatched away the lodestone. The needle stopped circling and settled in a north-south direction.

By the 1300s Italians in coastal cities earned their living from the sea. The richest men were merchants and shippers. They were always interested in new ideas for better navigation. On board every ship were books of sailing instructions called *portolanos*. The portolanos held maps called *portolan charts*. These maps were drawn on sheepskin and covered with lines to represent compass bearings. The lines reached out from the point

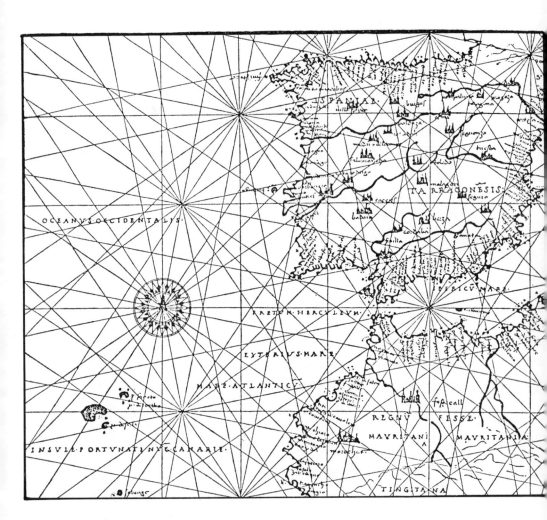

A portolan chart. Lines representing compass bearings reach
out from the wind rose.

of a star. Each point stood for a direction. Since ancient times people thought that the winds came from the four directions. The star looked like a flower with 32 petals. For these reasons the star was called the *wind rose.*

Chart-makers painted wind roses in beautiful colors, but their beauty had a purpose. Pilots often read their maps by dim lamplight. Colorful star points were easier to see.

The eastern point of the wind rose was marked by a cross. A triangle, dart, or the fork of the sea god marked north. Later, a French flower called a fleur-de-lis was painted above north. To this day map- and compass-makers use a fleur-de-lis to mark north.

Instrument-makers invented a dry compass by placing a pivoted needle above a wind rose. A round box protected the instrument. In Mediterranean ports sailors called the compass a "box." The first chore of a young seaman was to "box the compass." He had to memorize the 32 points of direction and say them in order, starting from north.

Around 1300, Italian instrument-makers invented the *compass card.* It was a wind rose painted on goose skin. A magnetic needle was glued to the underside of the card. The north end of the needle lay directly below the north point on the card. The compass card was better than earlier compasses because the entire wind rose spun around the pivot, not just the needle. It was easier to read than the old-style compasses, especially in rough seas.

Before the compass, Mediterranean ships sailed

only in summer. In winter, clouds hid the stars. With a compass ships could sail the year round, carrying more cargo and earning more money.

Every mapmaker drew a different wind rose on his portolan charts. Note the years they were made.

1384

1462

27

1520s

PRINCE HENRY THE NAVIGATOR

Sailing the Seven Seas

IN THE 1400s European armies were strong enough to drive the Arabs out of southern Spain and France. Many Arabs, and the Jews living among them, stayed behind. The Christian Europeans cared little for unbelievers, but they left them in peace. This was wise since the Arabs and Jews were the best map-makers and instrument-makers in the world. Their skill helped European fleets rule the high seas and explore distant lands.

Prince Henry of Portugal dreamed of sailing to far-off lands. He longed to turn his poor, small country into a rich sea power. Travelers returned to Portugal with tales of African gold. Rivers of jewels and spices waited for anyone brave enough to find them.

Prince Henry knew his country's fortune lay in

Compass card with oval needle

trade with Africa. How could he reach those distant shores? Land travel was slow and dangerous. A sea route was the answer, but the Atlantic was an ocean of terror. Legends warned of a Sea of Darkness to the south. Though many people doubted these stories, their ships seldom left the Mediterranean. To risk open ocean they needed better compasses, maps, and other tools.

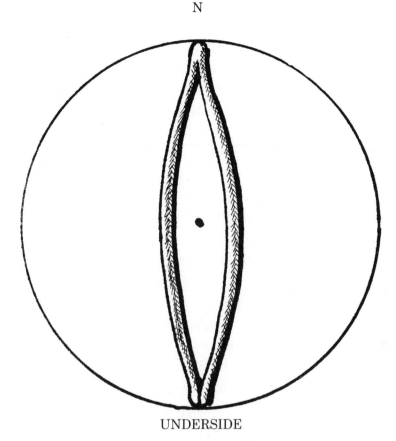

N

UNDERSIDE

Prince Henry vowed to provide those things. In 1419 he built a castle in the fishing village of Sagres. He called together the best instrument-makers, map-makers, and seamen to teach and learn.

The men at Sagres studied all there was to know about the compass. The instrument they devised had two needles instead of one. The needles touched at both ends forming an oval. The magnetized needles were placed on the underside of a card. A nail passed through the space between the needles. The compass card and needles spun around the nail until the needles pointed north. This compass worked well. The only trouble was that careless compass-makers often magnetized one needle more strongly than the other. The stronger needle unbalanced the compass so that readings were wrong.

Early mariners took bearings on an open deck. High winds and breaking waves ruined their compasses. Prince Henry's men protected their instruments in a glass case called a *binnacle*. The binnacle held an oil lamp so that on dark, stormy nights pilots read their compass dials by lamplight.

Seamen mounted the compass in *gimbals* before they placed it in the binnacle. Gimbals are two brass rings, one inside the other. They are fastened together so they can swing up and down. When the ship rolls from side to side, gimbals swing in the opposite direction. They keep the compass level, even in heavy weather.

The compass was an important tool for drawing maps. Fifteenth-century maps were full of mistakes. Oceans appeared smaller than they really were, islands were drawn in the wrong place, and continents were the wrong shape. Prince Henry ordered sailors and map-makers to work together. Their new maps told seamen exactly which compass course to follow. They marked the location of dangerous rocks and showed which tides ran along the coasts. The charts drawn at Sagres were

Gimbals surrounding a compass

CHRISTOPHER COLUMBUS

an example for other map-makers. A good chart saved many ships from crashing on rocks or becoming lost at sea.

Prince Henry was rewarded for his leadership. By 1450 Portuguese ships sailed up and down the African coast. Trade in spices and gold made Portugal a rich and powerful nation. The Portuguese gained more than riches from those voyages. They became the best navigators in Europe. The people of Portugal were grateful to their prince and the wise men he brought together. To this day he is remembered as Prince Henry the Navigator.

Sixteen years after Prince Henry's death seven ships battled off the coast of Sagres. A wounded sailor was washed ashore. He was an Italian from the seafaring city of Genoa. His name was Christopher Columbus.

Columbus settled in Sagres, learning all he could about navigation. Years later he tried to convince Dom Joao II, king of Portugal, that the Atlantic was a narrow sea. In a week's time he was certain to reach Asia. The king's advisers knew the world was larger than Columbus claimed. They turned him down and Columbus left for Spain. For six and a half years Columbus pleaded his case before Queen Isabella. Just as he was about to give up and try his luck in France, the queen granted his wish. She gave him three ships and orders to trade with China.

Columbus never guessed that America blocked his path. His skill lay in navigation, not geography. He chose a route that was free from calms, storms, and rough seas.

A compass guided Columbus across the ocean. One night he saw that the needle no longer pointed to the North Star. In his day declination was understood. Seamen knew that magnetic needles point a little east or west of north. But they didn't know that the needle's position shifts as the compass travels around the world. Columbus discovered that magnetic needles give different readings in places hundreds of miles apart.

By the early 1500s Europeans guessed why declination changes over distance. Lines of force flow from the magnetic North Pole to the magnetic South Pole. Some lines of force are stronger than others. As ships cross lines of force, their compass needles shift direction.

In 1519 a Portuguese sea captain named Magellan set sail under the Spanish flag to voyage around the world. Like many explorers, Magellan thought magnetic lines of force were separated by equal distances. He tried to prove that they flowed in great circles around the earth. Magellan was wrong. Lines of force bend in all directions. Some are close together and others are far apart.

Columbus and Magellan opened the way to the New World. Spain sent soldiers to conquer the Indians and take their riches. Gold from America poured into the Spanish treasury. Spain could then afford to build the greatest navy in the world. But Spanish power didn't last forever. The English wanted a share of the

FERDINAND MAGELLAN

37

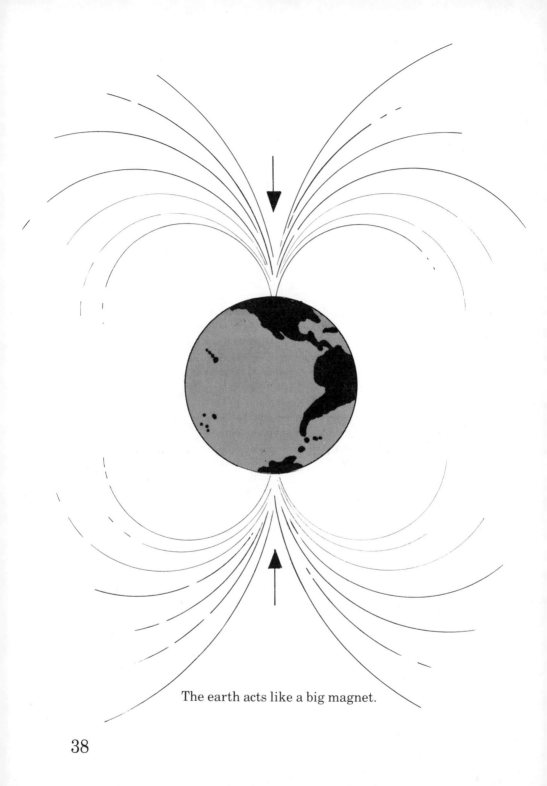

The earth acts like a big magnet.

new wealth. They built better ships and became master navigators. As early as the mid-1500s English pilots were experts with the compass.

In 1581 an Englishman named Robert Norman wrote a complete guide to the compass. As a young man Norman worked as a navigator. After twenty years at sea he chose the life of an instrument-maker.

Norman made a compass by balancing a needle on a pivot. Then he removed the needle and rubbed it with lodestone. When he returned the needle to the pivot it no longer balanced. The north-seeking end dipped down.

Norman experimented to find out what caused *dip*. He discovered that an "attractive power on the earth" pulled the needle downward. The power is the earth's magnetic field. At the equator, lines of force are parallel to the earth's surface. At the magnetic North and South poles they flow straight up and down. In between the equator and the two poles, lines of force are at an angle to the earth's surface. This angle is called dip.

Magnets line up with the earth's magnetic field. At the poles compass needles point straight down. At the equator they lie perfectly level. Between the equator and the poles magnetic needles point downward at an angle to the earth's surface.

Robert Norman was interested in everything about the compass. He described different kinds of lodestones and he made the first clear drawing of declination. Today, diagrams like Norman's appear on maps.

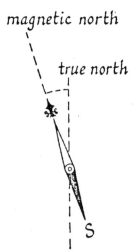

magnetic north

true north

S

Robert Norman's diagram of declination.

They give the exact amount of declination for the area pictured on the map.

Norman warned seamen about different kinds of compasses. English instrument-makers corrected their compasses for declination. They glued the north-seeking pole of the needle a little to the east of the north point on the compass card. In Italy compass-makers made no correction for declination. They placed the north-seeking pole of the needle directly below the north point of the card.

Both compasses were fine instruments, Norman explained. But pilots should never use an Italian compass with an English chart. English maps were drawn with English compasses and Italian maps were drawn with Italian compasses. Many ships sailed off course because they mixed the map of one country with the compass of another.

Robert Norman's good friend was William Borrough, an English Navy officer. When Borrough was young he pioneered a sea route from England to Russia. He taught himself map-making and became an expert at finding declination.

Borrough practiced finding declination at a place called Limehouse. He knew that declination changed over distance but thought that it stayed the same over time. Borrough couldn't have known that declination changes from year to year. The changes are so small that it takes twenty years for them to be seen on compass dials.

Fifty years after Borrough recorded the declination at Limehouse, a scientist named Henry Gellibrand took his own readings. Gellibrand's figures were different from Borrough's. Henry Gellibrand discovered something that the Chinese had known for centuries, that declination shifts over time as well as distance. Magnetic lines of force travel slowly around the world. Strong lines replace weak ones, changing compass readings.

Queen Elizabeth's doctor, William Gilbert, spent a great deal of time and money experimenting with

WILLIAM GILBERT

lodestone. Gilbert knew that opposite poles of two magnets attract. He decided that the south pole of a magnet points to the North Pole of the earth because the earth "acts as a great magnet." Gilbert tested his ideas by carving a chunk of lodestone into a ball. He called this ball a *terella*, which means "little earth." Gilbert tied one end of a thread to the center of a magnetic needle. Holding the other end of the thread, he passed the needle near the terella. When the north end of the needle dipped down, Gilbert marked the terella's south pole. When the south end of the needle dipped down, Gilbert marked the terella's north pole.

Gilbert believed that tall mountains caused declination. He carved a new terella with mountains and oceans. When he passed his magnetic needle around the terella, it pointed towards the mountains. Gilbert was certain that mountain ranges pulled compass needles away from a north-south position. But a lodestone terella is not the same as the earth. Even though William Gilbert was wrong about declination, his work was still important. For thousands of years people knew how magnets behaved but they did not know why. William Gilbert was the first to suggest that magnets point in a north-south direction because they are attracted to the earth's magnetic poles.

English pirates in the 1600s were experts with the compass. Seamen from every country feared their black flag with its skull and crossbones.

Sir Francis Drake, the buccaneer, was the pirates' worst enemy. Buccaneers stole only from Spanish

FRANCIS DRAKE

ships, sharing their treasure with Queen Elizabeth of England. Drake raided Spanish ports, taking maps as well as gold. When the Spanish navy tried to catch him, Drake fled across the Pacific. Only one other European had done this before, Magellan.

By the end of the 1600s England ruled the high seas. English navigators knew that declination changed as they sailed across the ocean. But they didn't know when it changed or by how much. They needed a map to give them this information.

The English navy hired Edmund Halley to draw this map. Halley was an astronomer, not a sailor. His crew hated taking orders from a "landlubber." In spite of

A declination chart for the year 1947.

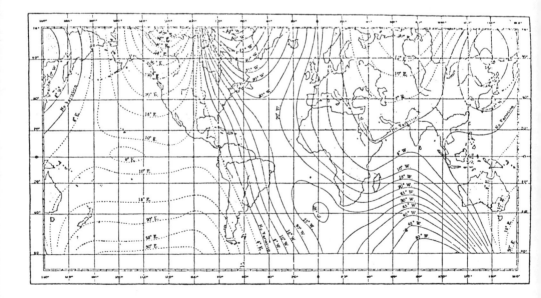

Halley's troubles, his voyage was a success. With his compasses, he mapped the lines of magnetic force all over the world. This map was called a *declination chart*. In time every large ship carried one of these charts. Halley knew from Henry Gellibrand that his map would soon be out of date. Declination changes as time passes. New charts must be drawn.

New Compasses and

New Problems

WITH BETTER MAPS, navigators needed even better compasses. Gowin Knight, a doctor practicing in London, discovered how to strengthen the magnetism in compass needles.

Before Knight's time, instrument-makers simply rubbed both ends of a needle with lodestone. Around 1745 Knight found another way. He discovered that many magnets tied together were stronger than just one magnet. Knight used his bundle of magnets to rub an iron bar and create a super magnet. He used super magnets to magnetize compass needles.

Knight called his system of making compass needles the "double touch" method. He wouldn't tell anyone how he did it, hoping to grow rich from the sale of

Dr. Knight's compass with a super magnet attached to the top of
the card.

48

strong magnets. His hard work paid off. Soon Knight became famous as an expert on magnetism. When lightning struck the battleship *Dover*, the British navy called on Knight to fix its compasses. The lightning flash demagnetized most of the compass needles and caused others to switch poles. The navy had put new compasses on board but they were also incorrect. Knight discovered that the binnacle was nailed together with iron spikes. The spikes had been magnetized by the lightning, causing the compass needles to point away from north.

Doctor Knight studied compasses from all over Europe. He found something wrong with each one, so he set out to invent a compass of his own. Knight attached a super magnet to the top of the card.

Knight's super magnet made a fine compass needle when the seas were calm, but it was unsteady in bad weather. British ships carried Knight's compass for eighty years. Finally, in 1837, the navy replaced it with the *Admiralty Standard Compass*.

The Admiralty Standard Compass was invented by a group of scientists, not just one person. It had four parallel needles. Two long ones were attached near the center of the card and two shorter ones were on the outside edge. The magnetic fields of four needles work together, keeping the compass steady in the roughest seas.

After 1850 all ships in the British fleet were made of iron. Compasses became inaccurate because of magnetic *deviation*. Every piece of iron holds a small amount of magnetism. Deviation happens when iron attracts compass needles, drawing them away from a north-south position.

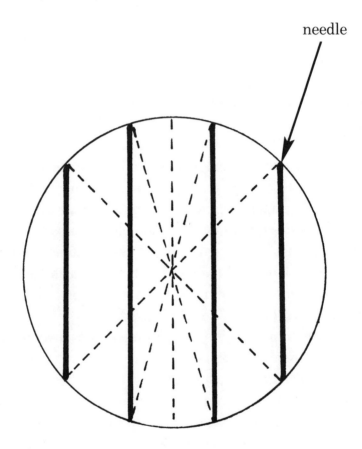

needle

Position of the four magnetic needles on the Admiralty Standard Compass card.

Experiment

DISCOVER DEVIATION

Make a floating compass with a magnetic needle, a cork, and a bowl of water. Put your magnet near the outside of the bowl. Does your needle still point north? Next put a hammer near the bowl. Does anything happen to the needle?

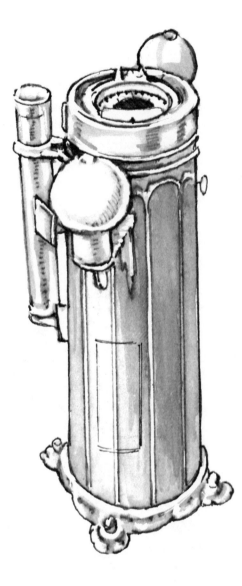

Lord Kelvin's binnacle

For hundreds of years deviation was not a big problem. Ships were built of wood. Many seaman didn't know about deviation at all. Captain Bligh kept his pistols in the binnacle. Even Captain Cook, the great scientist and explorer, put iron keys in the binnacle.

Lord Kelvin learned that small magnets surrounding the compass corrected deviation. He invented a binnacle shaped like a wooden tube. Inside were racks for corrector magnets. Lord Kelvin's binnacle is used to this day.

By the early 1900s all dry card compasses were out of date. Navigators turned to the liquid compass, an instrument used by the Phoenicians and the Chinese thousands of years before.

Sailors told an old story about a compass with its glass smashed in a storm. Its bowl filled with sea water. The navigator found that the water steadied the compass card as the ship tossed up and down.

Seamen knew about the liquid compass, but it took scientists many years to make one that was useful. They learned to mix water with alcohol to prevent the liquid from freezing. They sealed the compass bowl with rubber to stop leaks. And they invented strong paints so that markings wouldn't flake away in alcohol.

The first airplane pilots didn't need a compass because flights were short and close to the ground. Then came World War I. Bomber pilots flew back and forth across the foggy English Channel. Their airplanes carried a flat, liquid compass. Pilots took bearings by looking down through a glass top. In midair

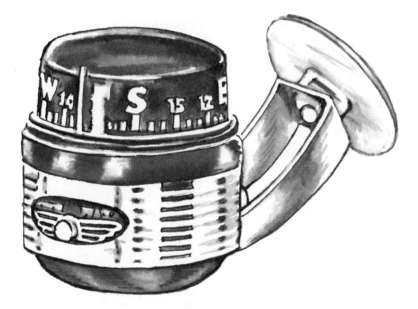

The vertical card compass

battles between British and German pilots, planes turned sharply in all directions. They would fly straight up or fall for hundreds of feet. The old flat compass was too hard for pilots to read and see ahead at the same time.

When the Americans joined the war in 1917, they used a *vertical card compass*. The card was shaped like a tube and spun around on a pivot. The vertical card was easy to read, even if the pilot flew upside down.

The British followed the Americans, putting a vertical card compass in all their aircraft. Each time a British plane crashed behind enemy lines, German pilots raced to the scene. The Germans knew that vertical card compasses were better than their own instruments. Every pilot wanted a British compass in his plane.

In the North Atlantic, battleships sailed with over one hundred compasses on board. Each one had a special purpose. They were used for steering, radar, and guiding torpedoes. It was impossible for navigators to correct all those compasses. Instead, an electric compass system made their job easier. The main compass sent electrical signals to all the other compasses on board. The signals caused every compass to give the same reading as the main compass. This meant that navigators had only the main compass to correct.

Modern Compasses

AT THE NORTH and South Poles magnetic compasses cannot be corrected at all. Lines of force are too close together causing magnetic needles to point in all directions. The poles are covered by snow and ice. Europeans couldn't find their way until they had a tool to tell direction. In 1823 Captain W. E. Parry explored the Arctic waters of northern Canada. A *sun compass* guided his ship. One hundred years later Commander Richard E. Byrd made the first flight over the North Pole. He also used a sun compass.

A sun compass is not magnetic. It is built like a clock with an hour hand to show the time. A pin stands straight up on the face of the clock. Explorers move their compass dials so that the pin casts a shadow over the hour hand. In that position, the twelve o'clock mark points north.

The sun compass works only in bright daylight. Roald Amundsen, the second pilot to fly over the North Pole, navigated with a sun compass until a snow storm put it out of action. Skillful flying and good luck saved Amundsen from crashing into the ice. At the poles storms blow the year round. The winter months bring total darkness. Like ancient Greek sailors, polar explorers could only tell their direction in fair weather. In storms and darkness they were lost.

An American named Elmer Sperry built the first *gyrocompass*. It was a tool that worked day or night, anywhere on earth. When a gyrocompass is pointed

A gyroscope

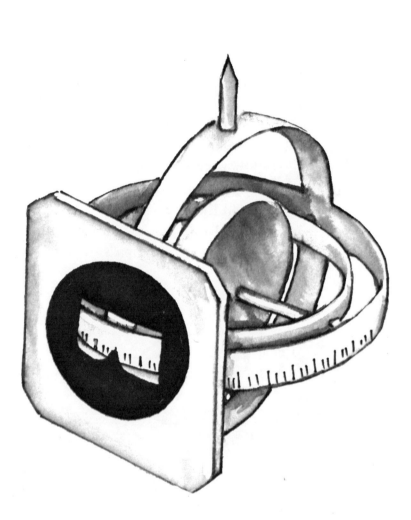

A gyrocompass

north it holds that position because it is made from a *gyroscope*—a spinning wheel set in gimbals. An electric motor spins the wheel, and the wheel turns in the same direction unless the position of the gimbals is changed or the motor shuts down.

In 1912 Sperry put four gyros in a plane to make the first automatic pilot. The gyros kept the plane on a straight and level course. Several years later he used his automatic pilot in an air torpedo. An air torpedo is an airplane that needs no pilot. The torpedo could hit a target fifty miles away. It was the first guided missile.

By 1935 many pilots used gyrocompasses instead of magnetic instruments. The old floating compass was unsteady in rough weather. When the airplane turned, the card spun around and around. Seconds passed before it gave an accurate reading. The gyrocompass held its position, even in the sharpest turns.

Battleships, submarines, and rockets need gyrocompasses. When the U.S. submarine *Nautilus* crossed under the North Pole, navigating for hundreds of miles below the ice fields, it was guided by a gyrocompass. The earth's magnetism had no effect on the submarine's compass because a gyrocompass is built without magnets.

The magnetic compass is useless in outer space. There are no magnetic poles to pull the needle in a north-south direction. The astronauts are weightless. They cannot sense the direction or movement of their spacecraft. The gyrocompass helps them navigate. Long ago sailors steered by the stars. Today the gyrocompass lets space explorers steer toward them.

The compass is a very old invention. Magicians, sailors, and scientists all had a hand in its creation. The compass gave people the freedom to travel further than they had ever dared, changing their lives and the history of the world.

INDEX